Love Sages

A collection of poems about love and hope.

Cover image © by Konrad (Conrado) Bąk, 2011

Printed in the United States of America

ISBN-13:978-0615515519

ISBN-10:0615515517

T.S.Garp

Acknowledgments

This is an acknowledgment to all the poets, people, and themes that have inspired me to write, pursue, and create poetry about the mysterious qualities of love. Love Sages is dedicated to Sara, Jennifer, Debbie, Claudia, Tatiana, Alexandra, and Kathy. With inspirational themes about attraction, coincidence, love, romance, happiness, hope, renaissance, reflections, immortal, friends, dreamers, paradise, holidays, nature, sensuality, fears, passion, soulmates, and the works of Edgar Allan Poe, H.P. Lovecraft, Oscar Wilde, and William Blake

A collection of poems about love and hope.

Loves Sages

by

T.S.Garp

Clarity's Love

All I know is that life is forever changing
All I know is that this is so astounding
All I know is the world keeps spinning
All I know is this time is so rearranging

All I know is that I want to say hello
All I know is that we ought to save and show
All I know is that I want you to know my name
All I know is this life is never quite the same

All I know is how life unfolds
All I know is the way we roll
All I know is how strange it is
All I know is wow what makes it this

All I know is how to love
All I know is how God is above
All I know is what is true
All I know is I need you

All I know is what is right
All I know is follow the light
All I know is this life is a painting of mine, see
All I know is that you are so loving and kind, to me

All I know is what is true inside
All I know is that is you in my alluring eyes
All I know is how lovely a touch can be
All I know is how I feel when you stand next to me

A collection of poems about love and hope.

Cupid

Oh, Cupid…
Hear me true

This will not take long,
I want to say to her, "I love you"

You know I can do…….
You know I will be true……

Cupid, god of love. I know your are there!
Come and please, and answer my prayer!

She is so beautiful, and if you saw her you would know too
Oh, Amor! Come help chase away these blues

I want tell to her this love is so true
The Greeks may call you, Eros!

Oh, Cupid! I know it's you!
So shoot your arrows true!

She is so pretty and cute…….
I want to tell her but my voice is mute

Oh, Cupid. I know you can help me true!
So I send this message of love to you!

Blue Moon

I sat under the stars at night
Surrounded by mountains and trees

You held my hand,
and everything felt so right

I was consumed with love,
and something came over me

I looked up to see,
in my dizzy state of mind

The bright blue-silver moon,
glimmering through the trees far above

For this precious moment,
only happens once to some

And I knew this was no ordinary kind of love
Bodies meshing into one

Under a blue moon and stars so bright
Kissing until dusk was done

A collection of poems about love and hope.

Loving You, My Soulmate

How could the dream come true
Standing here lost without you
All remarkable journeys begins with two
As our hearts sing that happy tune

In your eyes made of love
So deep, that shines so bright,
A beautiful gift from above,
A deep candle light, in the middle of night

Wondering through this time, seeking love
Adrift in an open sky, sailing by
Searching across the seven seas,
I have waited for thee

Guiding me to a beach of peering dreams
To your paradise, walking on white sands
That breaks gently between my hands
Greeting me into your loving arms

Holding this beautiful spark, this dream, this love,
Standing still as smiles wash over our faces
Blossoming hearts making a faithful start
Under the endless shimmer of friendly stars

Loving, breathing, enveloping you
These pleasant feelings are incredibly true
Knowing this love is here and right
Because it is happening to me this very night

Giving me hope for the future to see
A real dream to have and hold
That makes me believe in magic of old
That love is real and standing right in front of me

T.S.Garp

With This Red Rose

With this rose I give you my heart
You had me from the very start

Your smile makes me dance and sing
Your eyes tell me how happy it will bring

Your gentle touch drives away all my blues
Your sweet voice lifts up my mood..........

And I see the true you.....with eyes so full of love
This must be surely a gift from above

For heaven knows.......
I've been looking for you my dearest

Holding on to that dream,
and melody inside my head so cherished

You are everything I want in this world so true.......
You are my miracle and there's no one else but you......

So take my hand
And kiss me now as only you know how

A collection of poems about love and hope.

Found My Way

I found my way,
I had to stop and say

I wanted to know, how long was I gone
The more I tried to understand this song

Never expected it to shine so quick and bright
Until I saw time past away under adorning lights

Between the clouds of my mind of uncertainty
Between changes that come continuously

What began as a start of emotion
Morphed into a pleasant rhythmic motion

There standing next to you,
closer now than I thought possible

A love that was lost from above
Found again on hands in the wind made so true

I wanted to know, how long was I gone
My mind spinning a dreamcatcher's song

The more I closed my eyes in a vertigo twist
My heart beating loudly whenever we kiss

Never expected this
Until I saw your lips

Eyes so sweet and hypnotic
A face beaming a smile so exotic

I found my way at last
To you

T.S.Garp

Kaleidoscope Of Dreams

Take your hands and put them in mine
Let's go spinning across time
Spreading the colors out and watch them shine

So sweet and dreamy, you pleasantly say
Running there without care making the whole day
Let's breakaway and live our way

You always make me feel alive and this way
So happy and high with you,
wanting it to last the night through

Don't you want to tell me why you want to sail
Soaking up the sun and wind in the free sky
Dropping our money in that wishing well

There is no time like this before and after
Sipping wine and song and enjoying it all
Tripping over ourselves with joy and laughter

I know you want to see these dreams too
For our love is made of everything you want
Holding hands together we can see it come true

A kaleidoscope of dreams swirling around us
Kissing made of soft sighs from the shakes
Made ever wonderful from your loving embrace

Kaleidoscope dreaming
Let go and start living
Arm and arm across a rainbow ceiling

A collection of poems about love and hope.

Holding Me

When I see you come near
My heart starts to sing true

Feelings of joy come over me
and I'm ready to slide away with you

You know how to find me there
I can see into your mind and hear

Taking us far on that cherished ride
Making all our dream come alive!

Always happens to us this way
Making the day shine in every way

Feelings so right and natural
Feelings so bright and sensual

Loving the love that I found this day
Emotions so high I can't say

Reaching out arms to hug me tight
Holding me strong until midnight

Taking my hands and watching my eyes
Kissing me ever so wide

Passion burning from this loving embrace
Made of our love's cool breath over our face

Mrs Passion Unexpected

In the middle of the day
She whispers sweetly,
that she wanted to play

With gleaming dark-eyes,
of a fiery temptress
She pushes me down......

Straddling me,
and gently says,
"I'm your princess"

Passion starts to hit the room
Love and sweet smells fill the air
As our temperature starts to bloom

She leans over with a smack
Making that French kissing sound
Sending me there at last tumbling to the ground

Out of breath and mind
Unbelievable sensation and time
Gentle rhythm motion in sync

Lost in thoughts and emotions
Feeling so blissful and sad
Selfish, I wanted it to last

A collection of poems about love and hope.

The Happiness Of Your Smile

She said I was her pleasant destiny
Without a second thought
She gave me her heart

Trusting her feeling so fine
Praying that I was a gift from above
To embrace a shared dream

The moment our smiles touched our hearts
Holding fast to that deep inner connection
We knew instantly that we could not part

She was happiest looking at my smile
Felt the love so straight and true
Not quite realizing all the while

There would be no other
That would come before or after that would do
That possessed us in such a love as this

From a timeless touch made sweet kisses
Our eyes dancing over our bodies in such bliss
Our delightful alluring smiles expressing all of this

Landing On Wings Of Love

Like a light shooting down from the stars
On wings of magic flying to you
My love arrived bold and beautiful

From out of the crowd of a million souls
Breaking from the pack from a life unfold
Catching my eyes, dark pearls that shine

Embracing, beautiful tasting our salty-sweet
Deep, penetrating silent greetings
Soft, wet, leaving my head spinning

Silky smooth fingers finding me at last
Affectionate arms clasping me tight
Aroma delightful with the sweetest scent

Bearing it all for me under a huge web-dome
Awakening, we escape the rush holding hands
Surrounded by strangers and travelers far from home

Expertly guiding me through the maze of people
Taking me to a transport of our dreams
Disembarking to cold and comfort

Near the walls of glass we gently hug
Staring out at the vast neon cityscape
Perched high in our castle of dreams coming true

Hands guiding me to reach you
From a thousand miles I disembarked
I came all this way to embrace your heart

A collection of poems about love and hope.

Love: Einstein Equation

Let's consider the equation of Love

Some say if flies in like a dove

That one and one, make two

No, my friends, that's not true

For love together make one

That equals out to the right sum

This is so true........

When you hear the words spoken softly, "I love you"

Morning Angel

My love has radiance,

shining, delicate, shimmering

in a skin made of whisp of lights.

Island In The Sun

I open my eyes
To no surprise

I see you there,
watching me with loving care

Silhouetted between bright and blue
Your magical smile bathed under the sky

Taking me in your waiting hands
Leading me there across the white sands

The sun slipping into a rainbow hue
Wasting the time away is so loving with you

So fine a moment is this happy emotion
As dusk came with stars gleaming in falling motion

Sitting close next to me by the fire at night
Your body wrapped in clothes of white

Passionate kisses stealing time
Your sweet breath inside of mine!

Your body moving up and down-
Secret flame burning higher and higher

Your kiss stealing my heart
Forever setting my soul afire!
From the very start

A collection of poems about love and hope.

Rhythm Lovers

Let the rhythm take us to lust
Surrounded by beautiful golden spheres of light
Kissing under the moonlight dust

Where the stars shine and dance for us
Spectacles of wonder gleaming by celestial hand
Having no end in this night in a sea of sand

No matter of mind or thought
Nor what hour it is can severe this trust
Hearts racing in tangent becoming one

Forever locked in rhythmic touch
Stimulating sensuous sounds heard
In tiny whispers made of words

Spontaneous motions natural and true
Wrapping our souls in a tangle of two
Knowing this love happens to a very few

Sudden and swift, a rising tide within us
Cascading and shimmering,
Overwhelming ecstasy in a rush

Rapture penetrating and hearts beating
Our souls merging simultaneously
Rhythm lovers are we, never ending completely

T.S.Garp

Waiting For You

In that dark place left alone
Some people call it home
I sit and wait under darkening skies
Thinking I let love gone tumbling by

Deep in the wilderness a cabin is sought
Isolated and alone without a second thought
Brought here by my lover's command

A flash of lightning catches my eye,
and a clap of thunder is close by
The weather begins to shift like my mood

Left alone again to sit under the blue moon
Now the rain is here adding to my tears
I sit waiting for you wondering what to do

I curl up by the fire for warmth at night
Staring at the fiery petals
Made of orange-crimson light

I entertain my wayward thoughts
With the silent language of contemplation
Feeling tainted dreams fade away

I'm sitting here waiting for you
How I wish my dreams would come true
Waiting for you to rescue me

From this isolated life left untouched
Cast aside neglected without so much
Waiting for my lover before I die

A collection of poems about love and hope.

My Love In All Seasons

The season's change with a quick glance
My love's attractive face remains the same
With a sparkling dark eyes that dazzled my mind

When the wintry ice finally melts away
My love's pleasant voice is ever present
With a majestic quality like no other

As springtime rushes in
My love's body moves in ballet precision
With a vibrant and exquisite grace

During the summer solstice heat
My love's burning heart shines on me
With pleasant words that set my soul aflame

As autumn winds blow gusts
My love's soft gentle hands never leave me
With an affectionate embrace that last all day

As cold winter rushes upon us
My love's Christmas spirit is my gift
With passionate kisses, I fall into eternity once again

The World Standing Still

When my eyes see you over there
Standing so sweetly with loving care
It's like the whole world is standing still

My heart all aflutter whenever I see you
Everything is so right and everything is so true
Especially when I'm standing next to you

Just the two of us
Soul to soul, heart to heart,
A promise of never being apart

White Sand Dreaming

When you dream of holidays
Your mind is lost in a haze

Filled with memories of the day
Postcards sent from an island far away

Telling our friends with happy notifications
With words of love and celebrated descriptions

So many greeting souvenir tomes
You want to stay there and call it home

Nothing matters anymore
But the sound of the distant shore

Looking out at the deep blue sea, together
Making you feel so happy, you want stay there forever

A collection of poems about love and hope.

Under The Stars With You

The stars shine so true
Made heavenward there for you
We come into this world of wonder
We travel in the wind made from dust
On the Earth to see each other

To see life unfold before us
To eventually breath a joy
To be loved night and day
To see the beauty of your face
To be happy at last feeling glad

So much to love and see
Let's take it all in and take hold
See with our eyes and hearts unfold
I promise to live that dream with thee
With you so dear, so much to me

Love So Near

Love is so sweet
When I see you talk
Right next to me
When I see you walk
Love is happier still
When the lights are out
When I know you are near and passion builds
From rapture sounds you make and shout

Love Requital

Watching the world go slowly by
Stealing my mind in this endless river of time
Washed away by storms from crying inside

I ponder until the night comes
Gray clouds sailing over my plight until dawn
I remember our dance in the soft moonlight

When will I see the oasis in your eyes
Take me from this desert view so dry
I need your sweet love to make me alive

Living in a world gone mad without you
Take me back to that bright ocean blue
Watching the tide break into white foam,
bathing over our hearts and soul so divine

Holding back the rain and let the sunshine through
Reminisce our wayward lives and all that we do
We can dance again with without even trying too

A collection of poems about love and hope.

Journey Into The Sun

Landing in this tropical paradise
Far away from our simple life

A thousand miles from nowhere
Leaving the navigator behind without care

Sitting in such a place made for two
So mellow and fun with you

Bathing in the bright yellow sun
Making you and I want to run

You wish we could go exploring everyday
Making the days last all this way

Just walking with you and me
Across the vast aquamarine sea

An endless journey toward the sun
On our paradise island filled with fun

How I love you here
Making the time so romantic, my dear

The Encounter

Such beauty came to mind
As the sailor's eyes, met Arionna Kives

She stood by the dock, looking at the rush of people
All leaving in their own private flocks

The sailor, with courage he had grasp from the sea
Introduced himself with some expertise

Overwhelmed her of stories and legends,
ideas, and flights of fancy

All of which he claims to have seen
Enthralled, she was by his tales of extravagant encounters

Arionna Kives reasons were strictly one of pride
To take up with such a fellow,
whom to her had the most handsome color eyes

As the passage of time struck louder the years rolled by
Like dropping peddles from a flower

The man and woman despite temptations,
stayed true to their expectations

The church bell ringed! The cheering began
As the two newlyweds walked hand and hand

This is the end of their tale
We should think that it ended well

A collection of poems about love and hope.

Darling You

Darling you, wait a while
Let me see you smile

Stop and play
Look up at this wonderful day

Darling, you. Feel the season is true
Bright and blue. Sweet and nice

See all the splendor of life
Come on. Come and stay

Join me and come out to play
Darling, you.......

See this love so true
The sun is so high

The birds are all in flight
The love is so right

We're lost in paradise
Such a perfect day

You stop and say
I want to stay-

Forever with you
This is all I can do

Such a beautiful way-
Today!

T.S.Garp

Dreaming Of Gwynhwyfar

When I close my eyes lying here
In the middle of the day I can see you there
Under the shade of a big oak tree
I sit and ponder and wonder what will be

My soul was empty before you arrive that day
Contemplating and guessing my time away
Appearing suddenly she is gentle and fair
Blushing with a smile was my dear Gwynhwyfar

Behold this wondrous image in my mind
She leaves the essence of herself to remind
Gwynhwyfar's elegant voice sings with a magical tone
Made real with loving touch never leaving me alone

Gwynhwyfar's eyes sparkling a gleam of delight
Passionate hug and kisses that last through the night
Awakening without her during the early morning hour light
Left lingering an angel's sweet aroma she is no where in sight

A collection of poems about love and hope.

From A Love

Making this time in the month of June

Sun blazing through our hearts too soon

We didn't know where or how or why

We only knew that love was a river,

and we were riding the tide

Braving the meadow and mountainous terrain

Forgoing fear we sought to maintain

An adventure together into the unknown

From a love made of solid stone

Lover's Spell

She speaks near the fountain of dreams

Flowers in her hair thy angelic voice gleams

Once she looked at him it was done so well

A long life together from a lover's spell

Her Midnight Kiss

She arose in the night covered in silk
Her eyes dark pool diamonds
Gliding across the room like ghostly milk

Gracefully navigating in the dark
She opened the windows to look at the stars
Letting summer's wind into our den

She turned and she called my name
A smile of shame filled her face
She confessed that she wanted me from the very start

Her wet lips met my own
And my wondering hand found home
Our hearts ran fast, breath was hot

She wanted to weep at the need
Her desire was open and surreal
Was it wrong to embrace this love so real

She spoke softly assuring me gently
Kissing every part of me from head to toe
Reveling in the moment, revering me sweetly

Letting the waves of joy pass through us
Shuttering, shaken embrace of trust
She moaned uncontrollably too much

Feeding the soul with hearts and words
Through faith and vows
Creating our love here and now

In this magical moment of happiness
A beautiful dream come true all the while
She looked at me and pondered a smile

A collection of poems about love and hope.

Annabel's Ring

I had to journey far and wide
I had to leave my Annabel, good-bye!

To embark on a path beyond the Sun
To seek a fortune in a tidy sum

I plan to marry my Annabel true
I would travel across the world for you

Through dangers and unknowns I will
From lands full of wonder and ill

Completing my wayward journey for a golden ring
I hurry home to see your happy face smile and sing

Living by the ocean near the church tower
Our wedding was monumental top of the hour

Annabel's heart sings true
And my life's journey was all but through

Alicia's Declaration Of Love

Alicia came in with a frown
Looking troubled and down
Her blonde hair tattered and tangled
Her heart on her sleeve revealed and mangled
She wanted to go someplace away from this town
I took her by the hand to escape any sound
We packed a picnic and headed for the hills
Leaving behind all the rumors and misguided ills

Alicia adorned herself in a summer's dress
Beautifully blending in with nature's colorful flowers
I quickly found the place where we could stay for hours
High up in the valley on green grass we made to rest
She told me her troubles full of wickedness and despair
About scornful friends and family
Who disagreed with our current affair
Full of jealous hearts made amply

Alicia compared me to the master Edgar Allan Poe
Who's writing sang a sung so much told
Yet who died a poor man with a broken soul
Those down below, speak to her, tormenting Alicia's soul
She was plagued with words of hate and disagreement
Sinister clans full of plans held back her hands
Claiming her love for a writer whose age was twice
They feared a dreamer, who never had much in life

Alicia vowed not to listen to such
She agreed in trice that this was a bit much
No one knows true love until it happens
When your heart tells you to stop and listen
She held my hand leaving all doubt behind
She said our love was a gift from heaven and so divine
A serious romantic interlude, a kiss leaving a mark
Pressing my hand on her heart, true love, not a lark

A collection of poems about love and hope.

Never Let Me Go

Never leaving love behind
Cast away all doubts that hold time
Never saying good-bye through the years
Singing sweet harmonies with happy tears

I look to see magic in your eyes
Staring at me with no surprise
I can't explain, your so true
How the time came to find you

When you love someone so true
You call their name and say I love you
What a simple thing to do
A sweet song made for two

Reaching out for them to hold
An embrace that last 'till old
Never letting go this dream of ours
A love that rings so very far

Destiny Of Love

I opened my eyes and saw you
I knew it was a dream come true
From all the things you do

Making our love shine so bright
With a smile and eyes so right
An attraction so passionate from first sight

Coming to greet me with gentle touch
My dream lover singing a gentle song
With a care and manner making me blush

Standing next to me, majestically materialized
Cleverly made to happen purposely
Under a veil of destiny, I realized

No more solitude of life
No more contemplation in the night
Farewell darkness and breath in light

Taking my heart to the extreme
Making the days pleasant and endless
Loving you was like living a wonderful dream

Holding me in your loving arms so tight like a spell cast of love
Beautifully, mesmerizing, echoing in our hearts forever
We were in chime and inseparable like a gift from above

A collection of poems about love and hope.

Beyond The Glass Mirror

A love that spontaneously erupts
Whenever they see each other

She fills the air with a beautiful flair
Beckons his face and charm

Drawing each other nearer
To place their hands on that glass mirror

Taking them higher beyond the moon
Making them realize it isn't too soon

Overlooked, a love that was missed
Now grows so much more than this

Reaching past old fears and lust
With harmony and wisdom and trust

T.S.Garp

Christmas Carol Romance

Nightmares and dreams
Alarm clock broke the scene

Shaken and stirred was I
Images of strangers filled my worried eyes

All done overnight they came
Like a Christmas Carol of the same

I ran out the door, down the street Christmas day
I traveled far to reach her iron gates

She awoke, thinking of me now
Hearing a knock, her heart sang out loud

As she opened the doors to her house
Behold to my eyes, a princess of winter

Dear sweet woman,
beautiful miracle holding me tight

From our creation,
a cradle of love made ever so right

Our Christmas gift this day
Made from dream spirits they say

Who promised us a world filled with love
With a sweet vision of my dearest foretold from above

A collection of poems about love and hope.

The Light Of You

I keep thinking of the light of you

I keep waiting for the sun to shine through

To see the light across the valleys of blue

To see the light inside of you

Giving me hope and courage

Bringing the dawn to a new day

Breaking the old ways

Stepping out into something new and bright

Making a journey to a new beginnings and sight

Keeping Faith and Hope alive

Keeping dreams close by my side

Waiting to see if you arrive

Basking in the light of you

How I love you

When I see the light of you

T.S.Garp

Love's Journey

"A great man once said that no matter how love happens, when,
why, where, and with who, does not matter, only that you do
love, that matters."

What began as friendship like most
Sharing the time just like so many folks
Our love grew into something completely new

A common bond making us two
Feelings started to grow so natural and true
When suddenly I started to notice the real you

Down by the sea watching the white birds fly
Like a pleasant breeze coming over me I asked why?
With eyes so serene and majestic I breath a heavy sigh

Suddenly embarking on a journey with you
Never thought my confident would see me through
Who are you with promise and hope so dear?

I'm now waiting for you down by the pier
Let's elope, raise the sails, ready to disappear
No matter from where we were before

Life holds no more mysterious unseen
Wherever our love takes us only happiness brings
For we love the love that has come knocking on our door

A collection of poems about love and hope.

Moonlight Kiss

Seeing you there blushing so
Greeting me with a smile
As I hold your hand and kiss low
Watching the gleam in you eyes all the while

Let us leave this party filled with old
Your eyes a burning flame
A temple of love with breast so bold
I stare back with no shame

We linger into the night
Our love made happier from that loving sound so much
Under the shine of stars and moonlight
Beautifully next to me as you glow at my touch

Days Gone Past

Shedding many happy tears
From a time long past brings you near
We reminisce that the world is so right
Together, sitting with you tonight

The days are years gone by so well
Under sunny-rain-clouds birds do tell
With your soul-searching eyes you grab my arm
Happier and sweet you sing along this song

We have seen spectacle wonders that call
Pass through the starlight of dream of it all
We have whispered our joy and love so close
Soft-gentle words of love spoken the most

Urban Love

I was making my journey late at night
Under a thousand points of light

I ran into the tallest building
Up I went in the glass booth

Dazzling dizzy lights.
Thankful, I wasn't fearful of heights

Up, up, up, I went.
The doors opened and I could sense

A premonition you see
I knew subconsciously

That something was in store for me.
She was standing there, working with care

An angel working overtime in the summer's night air
An aura of beauty surrounded this delicate flower

Our eyes suddenly met
Locked into passionate power

From hearing her voice it was love at first sight
Inside this mighty glass tower in the middle of the night

A collection of poems about love and hope.

True Love Promise

They say never let love go

Never forget

How love was made

Never let it disappear in vain.

Waiting For Me

Wait for me

Wait and see, my dear Josephine

Wait for the dreams to plant that seed

Wait for them to begin again to grow

Like the wind blowing through trees

Growing a love that transcends time

Waiting for the moment to rise with the tide

To watch our sunshine of imaginings

Waiting for the feelings to bring spring

Bringing our hearts into dreams happening

In The Shadow Of Her Love

A dream long ago of her shadow
Locked away neatly into infinity
I remembered her loveliness like it was yesterday
A reincarnation dream made of thee

A time that should have lasted forever
Giving me a flashing smile and her heart now
She slipped into the crowd seen again, never
Saying, my love what can we do anyhow?

In the shadow of her love
I was walking about in a make-believe scene
She made my life believe in miracles above
Made of the past and future it seems

A fantasy world where I met her
Standing like a princess, posed, and fixed
Clad in white and blue, her body light as a feather
Offering any passerby a kind word with no tricks

She was pale, frail, and slender
Spoke softly with words that linger
Sung to an eager listener
Smiled easily, so kind and tender

Her eyes encaptivating held me spellbound
I approached her and noticed her golden ring
My mind was spinning all around
Big and circular and shimmering

We were held transfixed to each other
She was a bride to be in this dream of mine
But we both agreed, we would want no other
Left standing in her shadow of love so fine

A collection of poems about love and hope.

Twilight Party Of Love

My piercing gazed passed over her lovely form
Over her long dark hair,
and noticed again that she was fully adorn

With jade, sapphire, silver,
wrapped around her neck and wrist
Perfectly matching her clever wit.

Our conversation was full of taste
We were in that happy place
Ignoring the crowd of other people in haste.

But time stood still in our eyes
Met for a moment in this vast time
Locked together with supernatural ties

Smitten, I asked where did she came from
She said from far away beyond the sun
Where they bite gentlemen like me for fun

Leaving the party with this bliss for a moonlight walk
She held my hand and clung to her frock
We traveled across the estate's garden park

Under some dead trees of autumn we leaned on
The wind blowing heavy upon us,
she ignored this and kissed me deeply, on and on

The delightful kisses reached my neck
Passionately sucking my skin until it was done
A rushing of my blood sent me awake quick

The alluring damage was done by her lips
In the twilight hour before any terror could transpire
I was taken willingly and the bite set my soul afire

T.S.Garp

Soulmates Across The Waters

I followed coincidentally in that path that led me there
Unconsciously leading me past a thousand faces
But my eyes fell upon thee, not once, but twice

Clad in white, beautiful, sheer and delightful
Before the days could part between us
Beholding me in your love-light

Our words began in the day and ended at night
The radiance of her was delectable and bright
Her soul invoking the power of second sight

We talked some more and we realized that
What just came before was something special,
and clearly so much more

She looked at me with intense almond eyes
Full of joy and laughter,
and simply said, "Why?"

But she knew instinctively
Smiling sweetly, knowing it was true
That love comes, right out of the blue

Separated by a collision of stars, so sad is this
It took years of sorrow, faith, and time
To guide us back into our destine loving arms

Love is eternal and forever vanquish wayward souls
No matter how old or time or where you are
For true love will strike you from afar

Destiny may have other plans, you see
But thy love you found, will part not
It will always be, in your heart!

A collection of poems about love and hope.

I Sing For You

I sing my heart, I sing the blues
I sing for love, I sing for you

I play a tune, one or two, I give this to you
In hopes that your heart blooms

I sing a little song made just for you
I sing a tale about the love so true

I sing my heart for the blues
I play in my corner on the street just for you

Taking requests under the summer heat
Hoping the message gets through to you and we meet

I sing the blues because I love you
I sing a sad song, because that's all I can do

I'm in the music lane waiting for you
I get the chords right whenever I sing the blues

I want to sing a tale for you, my dear
A tune so very true, so sincere

I sing the blues day and night
I sing from my heart from dusk until light

This is my life this song
I sing it for you for what was done wrong

T.S.Garp

The Renaissance Affair

My love stood in view near the Castle
A happy vision of green hills and her pink tassels

The fire in her eyes so opened my heart
Making this old knight ready to make a new start

Throughout my campaigns treacherous journeys
Like a moth to a burning flame, I returned to her in a hurry

I labored and travel far, missing her soul next to mine
Returning from dark skies, now sunshine

My gallant knight,
she called to me silencing the battle roar
Tormented no more, reaching her sweet shore

It is true, that all that is due will come back to you
Let love guide you to that special one across the unknown

A gift that grew from a heart that must
See it there made before your eyes from dust

A collection of poems about love and hope.

She

She could see me
She could tell

She held the spell
She had done well

She held my heart
She had it from the start

She was an angel with dark eyes
She was too kind to hide any disguise

She was demure
She was an allure

She could see me there
She would stare

She could not look away
She stood still with dismay

She could...........
She would.........

She made everything good
She gleamed so pure

She felt she knew me before
She made love seem so much more

She delightfully laughed, surprised
She was happy at last, mesmerized

T.S.Garp

Dear Fantasy

A vision of magnificent mountains

Tallest trees, green grass, and a luminous lake

Standing, balcony, under magnificent towers

A time of immortal, a past, beyond this present hour

A magical moment to save

The two of us adoring this wave

Small dragons give praise and come out to play

We kiss, gentle ways, under the sunny day

My princess bright-eyed,

true in heart, who's love is deemed

Humble and sweet

A kiss that was made from a dream

A collection of poems about love and hope.

Wasting Time With You

"No time is ever wasted in matters of love, wasting the time is how it is done"

With the wind in your hair,
dangling through the warm celestial glare
I can see your eyes, pools of blue
Heavenly glance full of faith and true

Driving with you and walking too
Your laughter mixed with talking
The skies so free, open, and blue
Wrapping fingers in tow, how I love you

Wasting time with you doing this and that now
With my honey, as I kiss her gently on the brow

Let's soar high through the lavender air
Because we're free to do whatever we want without care

Spending time roaming here and there
It's true I found you and not a moment to despair

I wish all our days could last forever!
Wasting time with you, leave me never!

By grace of God she loves me so well
She agreed happily and felt her bosom swell

Our life is so real and bright at last
Faith walks by our side and corrects the past

Placing a ring on her finger from days of trances
She is so happy now sharing eternal loving glances

Specter Of Love

The castle of dreams looms ahead
And our love is eternal outlasting the dead

No matter what time or day
The hourglass can't steal away our play

We'll go on past this eclectic life's song
Transformed and see a new dawn

The endless walls of time will not hinder
Nothing will stop us from coming together

Our love eternal will rise again
Pushed forward by the seven winds

Even death makes us new once more
Metamorphosing, reincarnating our soul

We linger there between the land and the sea
Specter of shadows of lovers longing to be

For true lovers live on and on, never left alone
Still singing that courageous loving song of old

A collection of poems about love and hope.

Sweet Monica's Gift

Fashioned of beads around her neck
Twisted brown strands dangle down her thin shoulder
Falling gracefully upon her breast
Soft and delicate like no other, oh I wanted to hold her

Bright, bold, glimmering, to my surprise
The natural curvy of her smile
The sun's reflection bounces off those perfect eyes
Holds everything but denial

Picnic setting flowers bloom with a loving trace
Intuitively, gently, her hand touched mine in playful fun
Thoughts abound, a ponder look on her face
Gleefully she looks at me realizing what she had done

Wondering and waiting for those words spoken
Like a dream I don't want to be awaken
Hearing from her sweet soul that nothing is broken
My life is alive and my heart pleasantly shaken

In a voice so kind and sure, she whispers me a song
From a splendor of glory she had sung
A passionate tale, singing to me that I belong
Showering me with love and dreams not yet gone

Wallowing in sybaritic splendor, closed our eyes to rest
The air filled with lilac fragrance, let loose by petal's roam
Emotions high, kissing, sated, loving, hard to express
Dizziness, embrace, harmonic rapture, sending me home

Summer Moon

When the Moon is full
Our hearts begin to bloom

You move your body down
I see you there lying on the ground

Staring up at me full of wonder and kindness
You know not what you have found

Forever there smiling
Across a million years shinning

It is you! My dear love so true!
With eyes so sparkling and new!

Watching the orange moon glowing
Watching our glorious love flowing

The blushing moon stood silent
Never leaving us or going away

Locked in an eternity of emotion unrelenting
Embracing each other until the very next day

Holding me tight at midnight under the summer moon
Hearts beating a lifetime all the way until next noon

A collection of poems about love and hope.

Eternal Love

She came near with pretty eyes
Enveloping me in her aura sanctuary
She could see the future full of bright skies
Knowing this she kissed me passionately

Immeasurable are we with each passing century
Her ardor heart and loyalty staying with me
Our souls dancing and gliding to infinity
A love so rich and deep you see

Imagining how the love would be
From spirits of a life gone now speak to you
Let the sad wind blow over thee
Listen to the sounds of a life you make so true

With every new life transformed and created you do
Soul of splendor given a second chance
Reincarnated again is all happening anew
A human star in another form to make the last dance

Eternal love that never wavers or bind
Encapsulated souls in shells are we
My dear is charming and divine
Reminisce of love that dwells of thee

Giving me a thrill when I recognize you, my star
Together beyond the pillars of time making it forever
Ostentatiously so beautiful and sweet to me seen from afar
I drink your breath kiss of life that leave me never

T.S.Garp

Courageous Heart

The struggle of daily life's drama is murmured here
Filling the mind with doubt and despair in there
Look more clearly past confusion and see it all
Can't you see it so true my love wanting you to call

Just take a moment to make it that way
All it takes is a courageous step to stay
Make our dreams come alive from that cast
Picture it in your mind and make it last

Worry not of rumors from wayward lots
Never facilitate or fall into others plots
Ignore doubt and fear that plague you there
Let your heart be your guiding light and show you where

Let us run through our fantasies upon the bed
Drinking the nectar of our hearts flower
Let's soak up our love and shine this hour
Embrace the vision that belongs to us filling our head

Never doubt what is real and true
Your loveliness is deserving and due
Let the canopy of clarity be in sight
Let passion-hearted love be your guiding light

A collection of poems about love and hope.

What Love Does

The hours sailed away

Adrift in the sea of time

Intoxicating rapture

Stealing hearts and minds!

Unexpected Love

We discovered our love
In different towns
Unexpectedly like a musical symphony
We heard the right sounds

Astonished by long-distance we were glad to be found
Her laughter was a breath of fresh air had me bound
There was no one else that compares to you
Over the time, days, months, and years coming through

Joyous happy seasons filled our time
Love growing, stealing emotions, was it a crime
She at first wasn't sure and made to trust
But as time soared she never knew love this much

No longer solitary as before
Her heart was content and assured
Feared disappeared and would not return to lure
She had found her beau, unrelinquishable nevermore

T.S.Garp

Reflections Of Love

A reflection of love so magical as this, near the bay
A timeless memory, she tenderly took his hand, as if to say
The birds and gentle breeze abound this day, welcoming sight
Beach flowers with colors so bright filled their hearts with delight

He looked at her so pretty, clad in her summer dress and hat
Holding hands she smile back at his handsome face with grace
Seashore walking with loving thoughts of past harmonies
Her body moved closer to his, clinging to his arm, soft and true

She embraced this time, with her love of life, so well in her mind
Her gaze adorn him as he took a stance on the seashore rocks
They stood and looked out to the vast sea, mother nature's gift
Romantic, shimmering, aquamarine liquid crystal of dreams

He began say, "Your eyes sparkle like the ocean's reflection."
She confessed, Your face and voice set my heart to beat."
He smiled wide and hugged her ever so much more
She smiled and said, "Kiss me 'til I fall to my knees, please."

Loving this moment down by the sea, a sentimental ritual of two
Five years gone and they realize no other love as this could do
She basked in joy and looked at her dream incarnated. Standing
over there, her Captain bright and bold, never fearing the journey

Pondering, she would have waited a lifetime for him to appear
Sandy came to realized this was meant to be after all
Most of her life had been situated under dark clouds
Until he passed her way, sudden and so gallantly on display

Together, arm in arm, they sat on the rocks, she said: "This is
wonderful. You are the reason I am here enjoying this. A love so
true, awakening in the day and pleasantly remaining until
nightfall's play. Forever lasting through our lives, I asked no more

A collection of poems about love and hope.

Run With Love

Hold me forever more, my dear

Blinding and beautiful you are thee

Wrapping your love and heart so near

Made especially and exclusively for me

Escaping frustrations and the dire motions of need

Holding and embracing our loving emotions with tears

Embracing all wonders and dreams and letting go of all heed

Dear heart sunshine break away and hold me near

Let us run together under the yellow sun

Reach out and take hold of my hand, thee

Discarding and shaking, off the day's trembles be gone

Leave it all behind and run with me

When Love Has No Rules

When passion takes over
There's no room for another

Like lightening it overrides common sense
Sending deep love penetrating our lips

A kiss so divine to destroy our minds
As two bodies rhythmically intertwine

Into a jigsaw puzzle made of salty-sweat
And smells of sweet love running down your neck

Such a sensuous tender moment
Of fire and ice is this

So strong emotions making a bed of life
Heavy with breath passionately-merrily

Two souls kissing dearly
In the dizzy blue-darkness of night

A love so intensely
A French kiss made so enthusiastically

An embrace, submission
Communication without omission

Sending chills
Sending thrills

Shivers down my spine
Making your heart mine

A collection of poems about love and hope.

Shattered Heart

Darkness befalls my soul this long hour
Have I missed a step and not seen the delay
Young, unforgiving, and emotional she may

Crying inside from the laugh and wondering will it ever last?
Trying to explain to her dismay this awkward way
Dying inside, my heart shatters like a glass

Pull me closer again and say those spoken words
Make it sweet and longer than before, so sure
Let's make love again and feel the surge

Roses are red and violets are blue
Don't let the wind take away my love from you, nay
Tears run down my solitude once more and say

A confession of love made too soon
A kiss that was gifted from the heart
Beauty glittering a light of love now gone

Torn apart within the hour of devastation
Hold back the salty flow of tears once more
Turning our love into shattering hearts of desolation

T.S.Garp

Waiting For Love Seasons

It's that time again
For the rain to begin
My hopes and dreams on this spring
Memories and words do sting

The time has come for me to see
To make it how I wish it to be
I see life unfolding in so many rearranges
People happily starting families making changes

Wishing for my love so true
Wondering just where to find you
The season of the year for those wedding bells to ring
Autumn leaves fall down all around and the happy couple sings

Holidays, bright and fun for some, but I have none
I sit and stare at the open fire wondering is it all done
My lonely heart beckons and calls out
I alone every year wanting to shout

The crowd of happy people quickly rushes in
And the season all around the world changes again
Come delightful fallen snow
Hiding my down thoughts, not wanting to show

It's that time again this New Year
Green and bright as springs sets in no more tears
Waiting for my new love to appear
Given life again as I push aside all fears

A collection of poems about love and hope.

When Love Sees You

The day is bright and new
My feelings are so true
The way you look at me all the while
Your happy smile

The dear gift you bring
Your sweet eyes sing
With love so strong and right
Holding me day and night

When you finally see me
Time stands still
Lost in vertigo, spinning wheels
Feeling dreamy whenever I'm with you

You say hello with words that know
Your face is so sweet and divine
Reminding me of all the great times
From pleasant yesterday's that came before

With a deep love so true
Every year as time goes past
Remaining, I see you there too
Memories of our lives and cry and laugh with you

Letting it transformed into something more and grow
Seeing the future with new eyes that grow old
Realizing when love sees you never hesitate at last
In the presence of love you must be able to ask

Let Love In

Every time I see you there in the light
I'm struck by such a beauty and aching sight

She comes in burning blush at me
I look deeply into the soul-searching eyes,
and knows that she loves only thee

Let love in my divine princess of the night
Let it keep you safe and hold you tight

For true love is never a lie
You know in your heart that it will survive

To the end of time
When love sees you,
and makes your heart shine!

A collection of poems about love and hope.

Dreams Are Alive

Its time for me to say
What I have found from this life
It took so many years to find
My dreams are alive!

Never saw it this way before
Never had a chance to see it
Never was privileged to be deep in it
Never recognized it until I saw your face!

Now I know that there's hope for me
My whole life has been less than it should
Something inside of me that knows true
My entire body is on fire when I met you!

Coming in so clear to rescue to me
Like spring flowers that glow at night
A love shining so bright on my deserted soul
My eyes light up when I see you there!

Here love is not crazy, but so divine
Here love is a wonderful feeling of mine
Here love is a reflection of our wayward lives
Here love is turning our dreams around!

Thoughts inside my head of this amazing love
Making me consider that dreams are real
A dear soul that holds me together
My tears of joy rain down on you and me!

T.S.Garp

How We Love This Life

Here we go again....
Let this dream take us away!
Bathing us into this light
Because this love shines so bright!

Here we go again....
I just want to say, how is this done?
I just want you to stay with me under the sun!
How I love, this life so much
How we hold, so tight and touch

Here we go again.....
Let the love in and see how!
Be in all this world as to say and see
Because your love is here to set me free!

Here we go again....
Making our dreams come true
Any moment or time, spending it with you!
Feeling so alive by your side, that we achieve
How this love brings this life, in perfect harmony!

A collection of poems about love and hope.

When The Rain Fell

The night sky's shadow is falling all over me

The clouds came to bring the sad rain around me

I thought I lost track of this loving feeling made of sunlight

Swirling in a mist of brilliant dreams now a sudden night

The light was so bright the day before, burning my face

Where did the sun go made of bliss, leaving its trace

Crystal clear rain drops fell, making its rainbow along the way

Clapping thunder shook to tell, threatening to take me away

The silver lightning blinded and penetrated me

The rain washing over me till I began to sing out happily

How could I be sad at this water blessing from thee

My life was empty until this rain epiphany came down blissfully

Now she came to understand what was done with clarity

No more tears of rain instead soaking me with your purity

Allowing true love to shine on me through raindrops made of

thee. When the rain fell this lonely day I knew love would fine me!

T.S.Garp

Sunset California

It happened one long hot summer's day

The bottom fell out and I had just had to say

When the ocean tide came in so clear

Washing out our sandcastles over here

Nothing to say except, "Sunset California" is here to stay

Her eyes were radiant like burning beacons full of play

Walking on Redondo Beach, heart filled with joy that whole day!

All my friends yelled, "Hey!" Across the Pacific Coast Highway!

I recall the seagulls, breeze, Briana and me

Her smile was wide, happy, and so free

I put my arm around her gentle waist and had to say!

We walked until dusk along King Harbor shore all day!

The ocean sparkling by moonlight this wonderful night!

Watching the LA horizon aglow like Christmas lights!

She made this celebration, chasing my blues away

She took my shaky hand and kissed me by the bay

A collection of poems about love and hope.

Under The World

Under the world of discover

She waited despairingly for her lover

Under dark clouds she stood there

Looking for a sign from some where

The rain hit her hard this night

Trying to drench her inner light

Standing over there waiting so long

Now she waits for her favorite song

A kind voice sings to her there

Filling her emotions asking where

Taking her out of this place

Making her feel that lost trace

Standing there under the world alone

Looking for answers to bring her home

As the rain poured over her tears

She promised herself no more fears

T.S.Garp

God's Favorite Ring

A conversation between lovers.

I say: It starts with the sun shining on and on until it goes away
Than the gleaming stars, bold and bright, come out to play
This happens every time I think of you, day by day

You ask me what are dreams made of? Where do they come
from? Where do they go when you wake up?
How do we make them real to the touch?

I answer: It begins when you leave the gloom and worries
behind, and the brightness of gladness has begun to take root in
your mind, as surely as the sun shines again in your morning
window every time.

You ask will love save me from falling, into the abyss?
When life throws me a curve, will I see the calling, or miss?
What if I can not be where I want to be across the open sea?

I answer: My hands are open to catch you and nothing will seem
so far and wide. When storms hit washing you down, the trick is
follow the tide. You get back up in time. That's the magic of being
alive!

You tell me this is an never ending song.
You say how can I see so beautiful and no wrong.
You wonder about the secret and have waited for so long.

I answer: When the dawn returns and begins a new day. When
the whole world is high on a divine pedestal on God's favorite
ring. When you set your gleaming eyes on me like an angel.
When your dreams come true! Look in the mirror and the answer
is you!

A collection of poems about love and hope.

In A Time So Right With You

In days gone by
In days gone past
In days filled with glad

In a year of hope
In a month of dreams
In days of delight

In a time so right
In a time so near
In a time so high

In that special place
In that magical state
In that tangible dream

In a wonderful scene
In a timeless setting
In a picturesque vision

In the land of the possible
In the land of the probable
In the land of the potential

In promises made
In dreams laid
In ideas fashioned

In that moment in time
In that place in heaven
In that sanctuary of hope

In A Time So Right With You
(continued)

In that hour
In that minute
In that second

In my arms
In my hands
In my soul

In your thoughts
In your sweet eyes
In your dear heart

In this wonderful start
In this beautiful creation
In this everlasting salutation

To you………………

A collection of poems about love and hope.

Shine Your Love On Me

When you shine your love on me
Our hearts intertwine washing over us
Gasping joyously and suddenly I see

When you shine your light on me
I can breath and laugh and just be
Everything is happy and free

When you shine your light on me
There are no more rainy days with you
No clouds can cover such a divine light made so true

When you shine your light on me
Embracing you majestically in arms of two
Awakening to see the dawning light with sweet you

When you shine your light on me
Take my hand, walk with me
To the path down by the sea

When you shine your light on me
I am never afraid of the dark or frighten
You are my beacon of love here to enlighten

When you shine your light on me
My destination is true that leads me to you
Forever guiding me there into you sweet loving care

Soulmates

Like a simple song

As old as time

Souls singing a happy rhyme

Instant friends that smile

A warm greeting all the while

Soulmates thinking alike

Connecting hearts that knew

Lasting the years through

Two souls saying I love you

A collection of poems about love and hope.

The Sensual Souls of Us

Sitting under the sky kissing you
A gentle breeze dances over your hair
Passionate eyes speak to my soul
An embrace that holds me close

Lips so divine, ignites a flame
Our minds swirl, uninhibited, vertigo shame
From a long lingering day's obsession
We drift fast to sleep overcome by passion

Daydreaming, under the tree of life
We had climbed the day before in search of more
Looking out at the vast world
We could see every direction to explore

Awakening to the sounds of birds at play
Delighted in our hearts and dreams we made
Our love forever, even while sleeping
We gaze into each other's face left beaming

Breathing in every precious instant
Each moment meant to last beyond our resistance
Making all our daydreams of love lasting
You say with veracity, wishing it to be eternally

From making our dreams into a reality
Taking us to that endless feeling of sensuality
We kiss again the whole day
Beholding our love in so many ways

Nothing is as great as this
Two hearts spinning in joy
and happiness

T.S.Garp

www.ingramcontent.com/pod-product-compliance
Lightning Source LLC
Chambersburg PA
CBHW060703030426
42337CB00017B/2748